A LITTLE BIT OF LADY GAGA

Copyright © Octopus Publishing Group Limited, 2025

All rights reserved.

Text by Caitlin McAllister

No part of this book may be reproduced by any means, nor transmitted, nor translated into a machine language, without the written permission of the publishers.

Condition of Sale

This book is sold subject to the condition that it shall not, by way of trade or otherwise, be lent, resold, hired out or otherwise circulated in any form of binding or cover other than that in which it is published and without a similar condition including this condition being imposed on the subsequent purchaser.

An Hachette UK Company
www.hachette.co.uk

Summersdale Publishers
Part of Octopus Publishing Group Limited
Carmelite House
50 Victoria Embankment
LONDON
EC4Y 0DZ
UK

www.summersdale.com

This FSC® label means that materials and other controlled sources used for the product have been responsibly sourced

The authorized representative in the EEA is Hachette Ireland, 8 Castlecourt Centre, Dublin 15, D15 XTP3, Ireland
(email: info@hbgi.ie)

Printed and bound in Poland

ISBN: 978-1-83799-881-4
eISBN: 978-1-83799-882-1

Substantial discounts on bulk quantities of Summersdale books are available to corporations, professional associations and other organizations. For details contact general enquiries: telephone: +44 (0) 1243 771107 or email: enquiries@summersdale.com

This book is unofficial and is not endorsed by or in any other way connected with Lady Gaga. Every effort has been made to ensure that all information is correct. Should there be any errors, we apologize and shall be pleased to make the appropriate amendments in any future editions.

TO

....

FROM

....

INTRODUCTION

Dear reader,

If you are a bona fide Little Monster, then there are a million reasons why you'll love this book!

Lady Gaga went from struggling New York arts school dropout to the edge of glory as a Grammy-winning household name in only a few short years, and such an extraordinary rise to fame deserves to be celebrated. From singing and just dancing her way to her first record deal, to dodging paparazzi, this book reveals how a star was born.

A Little Bit of Lady Gaga offers a fascinating glimpse into the mayhem, and a peek behind the perfect illusion of her stage persona. Learn fun facts and insider knowledge, keep your poker face in place while you test your friends at trivia, and be inspired by some of her most applause-worthy quotes.

It's time to celebrate your stupid love for this iconic pop star!

DON'T YOU EVER LET A SOUL IN THE WORLD TELL YOU

THAT YOU CAN'T BE EXACTLY WHO YOU ARE.

LADY GAGA

DID YOU KNOW...

The iconic name "Lady Gaga" was inspired by the hit Queen song "Radio Ga Ga". Although we don't know who officially came up with the moniker, Lady Gaga's then producer, Rob Fusari, apparently texted her the song title. His phone corrected "Radio" to "Lady", and the rest is history.

Although we know her as Lady Gaga, she was not born this way. What is her real name?

———

a) Stephanie Angelina Susanne Germanotta

b) Stefani Jeanne Angela Germanotta

c) Stefani Joanne Angelina Germanotta

I'M JUST TRYING
TO CHANGE THE
WORLD, ONE
SEQUIN AT A TIME.

LADY GAGA

DID YOU KNOW...

Long before she became a
pop star with her own music
videos, Lady Gaga made her
screen debut as a background
extra in AC/DC's music video for
their song "Stiff Upper Lip"
in the year 2000, when she
was just 14 years old.

In which famous TV show did Lady Gaga have her first acting credit under her real name, Stefani Germanotta, at age 15?

———

a) *Grey's Anatomy*

b) *The Sopranos*

c) *Law & Order*

Whether I'm wearing lots of makeup or no makeup, I'm always the same person inside.

LADY GAGA

DID YOU KNOW...

At just four years old, Lady Gaga began teaching herself how to play the piano by ear. Her mother, Cynthia Germanotta, asked if she wanted to take lessons, but the four-year-old was confused by the idea of tuition since she claimed to hear the music in her head. At seven years old, she started taking lessons that helped her learn to read music. The tuition clearly paid off because now she is said to keep her Grammy Awards sitting on top of her piano at home!

The Recording Industry Association of America has certified two Lady Gaga songs as diamond, meaning they have gone platinum ten times. Which two songs are certified diamond?

---

a) "Bad Romance" and "Poker Face"

b) "Paparazzi" and "Shallow"

c) "Telephone" and "Applause"

NO MATTER HOW MANY ACCEPT YOU TO YOUR FACE,

THE PERSON THAT REALLY NEEDS TO ACCEPT YOU IS YOU.

LADY GAGA

DID YOU KNOW...

Before she had her own music career, Lady Gaga was an intern at Interscope Records where she worked behind the scenes for several other artists. At just 20 years old, she was writing songs like "Hypnotico", recorded by Jennifer Lopez, and "Quicksand", recorded by Britney Spears.

Lady Gaga calls her fans Little Monsters. What do her fans call *her*?

———

a) Big Monster

b) Mother Monster

c) Thee Monster

SOME WOMEN CHOOSE TO FOLLOW MEN, AND SOME WOMEN CHOOSE TO FOLLOW THEIR DREAMS.

LADY GAGA

DID YOU KNOW...

Before her music career took off, Lady Gaga was a go-go dancer, and got her start dancing at a dive bar called St Jerome's on the Lower East Side of New York City, which was run by her then boyfriend. If you're thinking of popping by, unfortunately St Jerome's no longer exists!

In what year was Lady Gaga's debut album, *The Fame*, released?

———

a) 2006

b) 2007

c) 2008

I am my own sanctuary and I can be reborn as many times as I choose throughout my life.

LADY GAGA

DID YOU KNOW...

In April 2010, the music video for "Bad Romance" became YouTube's most viewed video, and in June of that year, the "Alejandro" music video became the first to reach 20 million views in just two weeks. By October, Lady Gaga was the first person to ever hit one billion total views on YouTube.

What is the name of the 2017 documentary about Lady Gaga?

———

a) *Gaga: Five Foot Two*
b) *Gaga: Five Foot Four*
c) *Gaga: Five Foot Five*

PERHAPS WE CAN MAKE WOMEN'S RIGHTS TRENDY.

STRENGTH, FEMINISM, SECURITY, THE WISDOM OF THE WOMAN. LET'S MAKE THAT TRENDY.

LADY GAGA

DID YOU KNOW...

Before it was released as "Telephone", the song Lady Gaga and Beyoncé collaborated on was called "Underground". There are lots of callbacks to early Gaga songs scattered throughout the video, including Swedish lyrics and Mickey Mouse ears like in "Paparazzi", and "Paper Gangsta" playing on a boombox. The video later won Best Collaboration at the 2010 MTV Video Music Awards, and earned nominations for Best Choreography and Video of the Year.

In 2012, Lady Gaga appeared in an episode of *The Simpsons*. What was the name of the episode?

———

a) "Lisa Goes Gaga"

b) "Maggie Goes Gaga"

c) "Springfield Goes Gaga"

I ALLOW MYSELF TO FAIL. I ALLOW MYSELF TO BREAK. I'M NOT AFRAID OF MY FLAWS.

LADY GAGA

DID YOU KNOW...

It was always clear that Lady Gaga was destined to conquer the world of performance and fashion. Her first ever performance on stage took place when she was about six, in her first-grade school play, where she created her own costume with tin foil and hangers. She continued to make eye-catching, buzzworthy costumes during her rise to fame, and in 2011 she was named Fashion Icon of The Year by the Council of Fashion Designers of America.

On what date was
Lady Gaga born?

---

a) 6 March 1986

b) 28 March 1986

c) 28 March 1989

Acceptance, tolerance, bravery, compassion. These are the things my mom taught me!

LADY GAGA

DID YOU KNOW...

Before proposing to Lady Gaga, Michael Polansky asked for her advice on how to do it. She told him to wrap a blade of grass round her finger – which is what he did. The blade of grass has been preserved in a resin ring, which she still wears. The proposal also inspired the song "Blade of Grass" on the album *Mayhem*.

What was the name of the first fragrance launched by Lady Gaga in 2012?

---

a) Fame

b) Applause

c) Monster

I'VE BEEN SEARCHING FOR WAYS TO HELP MYSELF.

AND I FOUND THAT KINDNESS IS THE BEST WAY.

LADY GAGA

DID YOU KNOW...

In April 2020, Lady Gaga helped organize the One World: Together at Home benefit concert in support of the World Health Organization during the COVID-19 pandemic. It featured performances from Lady Gaga herself, as well as other musical legends like Stevie Wonder, The Rolling Stones and Jennifer Lopez. The concert special raised an incredible $127 million which, according to *Forbes*, "puts it on par with the other legendary fundraiser, Live Aid, as the highest grossing charity concert in history".

On which album cover is Lady Gaga positioned in profile wearing a pink hat?

———

a) *The Fame Monster*

b) *Chromatica*

c) *Joanne*

THERE CAN BE 100 PEOPLE IN A ROOM, AND 99 DON'T BELIEVE IN YOU, BUT YOU JUST NEED ONE TO BELIEVE IN YOU.

LADY GAGA

DID YOU KNOW...

The song "Boys, Boys, Boys", written by Lady Gaga and RedOne, was inspired by the song "Girls, Girls, Girls" by Mötley Crüe. Gaga said, "I wanted to write the female version of Mötley Crüe's 'Girls, Girls, Girls', but with my own twist. I wanted to write a pop song that rockers would like." She has also stated that rock artists like Nine Inch Nails, The Cure and Radiohead were influential in the creation of her album *Mayhem*.

Which famous Lady Gaga song was originally meant to be on Britney Spears' 2008 album, *Circus*?

---

a) "Telephone"

b) "Yoü and I"

c) "Marry The Night"

You have to fail and then get better. Then you have to fail again, and then get even better.

LADY GAGA

DID YOU KNOW...

Lady Gaga's first acting role in a movie was in the 2013 action film *Machete Kills*, where she played the character of La Chameleón. For her performance, she was nominated for Worst Supporting Actress at the Golden Raspberry Awards. While others might have given up, Lady Gaga's determination and dedication to acting earned her a Golden Globe nomination just six years later in 2019, for her role in *A Star Is Born*.

At a concert in Montreal in 2013, which body part did Lady Gaga badly injure apparently while performing the song "Scheiße"?

---

a) Her arm

b) Her toe

c) Her hip

I DON'T FEEL THE NEED TO

PROVE ANYTHING ANYMORE.

LADY GAGA

DID YOU KNOW...

In 2011, comedy musician Weird Al Yankovic released "Perform This Way" as a parody of Lady Gaga's "Born This Way". After her management initially rejected the idea, Lady Gaga herself said she loved it, and gave permission for her song to be parodied.

As of 2025, how many times has Lady Gaga hosted *Saturday Night Live*?

———

a) 0

b) 2

c) 8

IT'S ALWAYS
WRONG TO HATE,
BUT IT'S NEVER
WRONG TO LOVE.

LADY GAGA

DID YOU KNOW...

In 2011, *Forbes* named Lady Gaga the highest-paid female musician in the world, worth $90 million, a total made possible by her album sales, endorsements and a world tour. In fact, the figure exceeded the combined earnings of that year's number two and three highest-paid female musicians: Taylor Swift and Katy Perry. Less than a decade later, in 2020, *Forbes* estimated her net worth at around $150 million.

What was the name of Lady Gaga's third studio album, released in 2013?

———

a) *Mayhem*

b) *Chromatica*

c) *Artpop*

It is your right to curate your life and your own perspective.

LADY GAGA

DID YOU KNOW...

Lady Gaga has a German-language quote from poet and novelist Rainer Maria Rilke tattooed on the inside of her left arm. It translates to: "In the deepest hour of the night, confess to yourself that you would die if you were forbidden to write. And look deep into your heart where it spreads its roots, the answer, and ask yourself, must I write?"

What is the name of Lady Gaga's beauty product range?

---

a) House of Gaga

b) Lady G Beauty

c) Haus Labs by Lady Gaga

YOU DEFINE BEAUTY YOURSELF,

SOCIETY DOESN'T DEFINE YOUR BEAUTY.

LADY GAGA

DID YOU KNOW...

Lady Gaga has a younger sister called Natali Germanotta, who is an accomplished fashion designer. She was Lady Gaga's fashion stylist alongside Kelly Porter for the film *A Star Is Born* and is said to have once dressed up as her famous sister for Halloween. In Gaga's music video for "Telephone", Natali makes a cameo appearance behind her sister when she is speaking on the phone in jail.

Lady Gaga was born and raised in which city?

———

a) New York City

b) Chicago

c) London

RULE THE WORLD!
WHAT'S LIFE WORTH
LIVING IF YOU
DON'T RULE IT?

LADY GAGA

DID YOU KNOW...

Lady Gaga has had the same vocal coach since she was just 11 years old. The nephew of legendary New York vocal coach Don Lawrence – who taught icons like Christina Aguilera and Bono – overheard her singing to herself in a New York department store and put them in touch. Gaga has said that she was singing "I Want It That Way" when the owner of the store "pulled me aside and slipped a phone number in my hand".

Lady Gaga says she loves a particular genre of movies and TV, and even finds them "relaxing". Which genre is it?

———

a) Romantic comedies

b) Horror and true crime

c) Anime

I believe that if you have revolutionary potential, you must make the world a better place and use it.

LADY GAGA

DID YOU KNOW...

A number of universities around the world have offered courses inspired by Lady Gaga, including a course at the University of South Carolina called Lady Gaga and the Sociology of the Fame, and a course at the University of Virginia College of Arts and Sciences called GaGa for Gaga: Sex, Gender, and Identity.

What was the name of Lady Gaga's Thanksgiving television special that aired on ABC in the United States in 2011?

---

a) *A Very Gaga Thanksgiving*
b) *Thanksgiving With Gaga*
c) *Lady Gaga Does Thanksgiving*

I'D RATHER BE
POOR AND HAPPY

THAN RICH
AND ALONE.

LADY GAGA

DID YOU KNOW...

Lady Gaga has talked about her struggles with bullying in school, and how this affected her. One of the nicknames given to her by a group of high school mean girls was "The Germ", in reference to her last name, Germanotta. Bullying was one of the reasons she started the Born This Way Foundation, with a mission to "empower and inspire young people to build a kinder, braver world that supports their mental health".

What giant object did Lady Gaga arrive at the 2011 Grammy Awards in?

———

a) An egg

b) A telephone

c) A cake

WOMEN ARE STRONG AND FRAGILE. WOMEN ARE BEAUTIFUL AND UGLY. WE ARE SOFT-SPOKEN AND LOUD, ALL AT ONCE.

LADY GAGA

DID YOU KNOW...

Lady Gaga's online influence is far-reaching. According to the Guinness World Records, from 2011 to 2013 she was the most followed person on X, formerly known as Twitter. As of 2025 she has an astonishing near 82 million followers on X, and over 60 million followers on Instagram.

As Lady Gaga emerges from a swimming pool in the "Poker Face" music video, two animals are there to greet her. What are they?

---

a) Horses

b) Peacocks

c) Dogs

Money can run out but talent is forever.

LADY GAGA

DID YOU KNOW...

Lady Gaga's Super Bowl halftime show at the NRG Stadium in Houston featured hundreds of light-up drones that formed shapes in the sky above the stadium. This was the first time drones had appeared in any Super Bowl, and the performance brought in an astounding 117.5 million views.

In the 2024 movie *Joker: Folie à Deux*, which actor co-starred alongside Lady Gaga?

---

a) Johnny Depp

b) Joaquin Phoenix

c) Leonardo DiCaprio

BEING DIFFERENT IS A TALENT. YOU ILLUMINATE WHAT MAKES

YOU SPECIAL IN THE SEA OF SAMENESS AROUND YOU.

LADY GAGA

DID YOU KNOW...

Lady Gaga has been rubbing shoulders with the rich and famous since she was young. She went to a private Catholic school in New York City called the Convent of the Sacred Heart with some other famous alumni such as Paris Hilton and her sister Nicky Hilton. Although they were in the same school, Lady Gaga has said that their paths never crossed.

Which fellow pop star did Lady Gaga sing with on the track "Rain On Me"?

———

a) Ariana Grande
b) Justin Bieber
c) Katy Perry

I FEEL LIKE IF YOU'RE A REALLY GOOD HUMAN BEING, YOU CAN TRY TO FIND SOMETHING BEAUTIFUL IN EVERY SINGLE PERSON, NO MATTER WHAT.

LADY GAGA

DID YOU KNOW...

In 2011, after 1,300 bids were received, a teacup used by Lady Gaga at a Japanese press conference was sold at auction for a staggering £46,000. The teacup has Gaga's lipstick print and autograph on it, and the money raised went to help young Japanese artists who want to study in the US.

Lady Gaga is godmother to the children of which famous singer?

a) Rihanna

b) Madonna

c) Elton John

For being different, it's easy. But to be unique, it's a complicated thing.

LADY GAGA

DID YOU KNOW...

Lady Gaga's Las Vegas concert residency at Park MGM's Dolby Live, formerly the MGM Park Theater, featured two shows in one; the first began in 2018, featuring her biggest hits performed with her signature theatrics, and the second began in 2019, featuring stripped back versions of her songs with tracks from the Great American Songbook.

Which mythical creature does Lady Gaga have tattooed on her left thigh, along with the words "Born This Way"?

———

a) A dragon

b) A unicorn

c) A centaur

I'M HALF LIVING MY LIFE BETWEEN

REALITY AND FANTASY AT ALL TIMES.

LADY GAGA

DID YOU KNOW...

Lady Gaga's iconic image inspired a world record! In 2011, a total of 121 people turned up at the Grammy Awards wearing Lady Gaga costumes. The result? A Guinness World Record celebrating the Largest Gathering of Lady Gaga Impersonators.

Which record label first signed Lady Gaga then later cancelled her contract before she released any music?

———

a) Def Jam Recordings

b) Warner Music Group

c) Sony Music Entertainment

EVEN IF THE
WHOLE WORLD
TURNS THEIR BACK
ON YOU, YOU
WILL ALWAYS
HAVE YOURSELF.

LADY GAGA

DID YOU KNOW...

Lady Gaga is said to have made some unusual requests at venues on her Monster Ball world tour, including an oxygen tank and some non-sweaty, non-smelly cheese. She also requested themed dinners for each night of the week, including a barbecue on Mondays, Mexican food on Wednesdays, and on Sundays… a turkey dinner with all the trimmings!

In which music video does Lady Gaga appear in prison wearing Diet Coke cans in her hair?

---

a) "Alejandro"

b) "Telephone"

c) "LoveGame"

We are equal.
We both walk
our two feet
on the same
earth. And
we're in this
together.

LADY GAGA

DID YOU KNOW...

Early in her career, Lady Gaga met fellow go-go dancer and DJ, Lady Starlight, at a Manhattan party. The two became friends and went on to collaborate on a number of projects including Lady Gaga & The Starlight Revue, a low-fi tribute to 1970s variety acts featuring synth, go-go dancing, and setting a can of hairspray alight while spraying it into the audience!

Which legendary jazz singer did Lady Gaga release the album *Cheek to Cheek* with in 2014?

---

a) Gregory Porter

b) Amy Winehouse

c) Tony Bennett

I DON'T CARE WHAT PEOPLE THINK ABOUT ME,

I CARE WHAT THEY THINK ABOUT THEMSELVES.

LADY GAGA

DID YOU KNOW...

Lady Gaga has said that she cold-called *American Horror Story* creator Ryan Murphy to ask for a part that would give her "a place to put all of [her] anguish and rage". This led to her being cast as the Countess in *American Horror Story: Hotel*. Despite the confident approach, she was apparently so nervous on the first day of shooting that she threw up in a bag on the journey there, and brought it with her to the set.

What is the name of the charitable foundation launched by Lady Gaga and her mother, Cynthia Germanotta, with the mission "to empower and inspire young people to build a kinder, braver world that supports their mental health"?

_____

a) Born This Way Foundation

b) Million Reasons Foundation

c) Edge of Glory Foundation

Why spend your whole life trying to be somebody that you're not? It's so much more fun to be yourself.

LADY GAGA

DID YOU KNOW...

When Lady Gaga sported her natural brunette hair colour, she was compared to Amy Winehouse. To stand out and create her own image, she decided to dye her hair the signature platinum blonde colour she is most known for today.

In which series of *American Horror Story* did Lady Gaga make her second appearance?

---

a) *American Horror Story: Murder House*

b) *American Horror Story: Freak Show*

c) *American Horror Story: Roanoke*

You have to be open to change to write a new era in your life.

LADY GAGA

DID YOU KNOW...

At the 87th Academy Awards in 2015, Lady Gaga stripped back the theatrics and paid tribute to Julie Andrews with a medley of songs from *The Sound of Music* in a performance that was widely considered one of her most notable. At the end, Julie Andrews came onstage to thank her in person.

Which song mentions the Alfred Hitchcock film titles *Psycho*, *Vertigo* and *Rear Window* in the lyrics?

———

a) "Bad Romance"

b) "Die With A Smile"

c) "Bloody Mary"

FIGHT AND PUSH HARDER FOR WHAT YOU BELIEVE IN,

YOU'D BE SURPRISED, YOU ARE MUCH STRONGER THAN YOU THINK.

LADY GAGA

DID YOU KNOW...

Along with writer Diane Warren, Lady Gaga co-wrote the song "Til It Happens to You" for a documentary called *The Hunting Ground*, which detailed the prevalence of sexual assault on college campuses in the US. The song earned them the award for Best Song in a Documentary at the 2015 Hollywood Music in Media Awards.

In which 2018 movie did Lady Gaga play the lead role of Ally?

———

a) *Sin City: A Dame to Kill For*

b) *A Star Is Born*

c) *Joker: Folie à Deux*

I THINK TOLERANCE AND ACCEPTANCE AND LOVE IS SOMETHING THAT FEEDS EVERY COMMUNITY.

LADY GAGA

DID YOU KNOW...

In a bid to get gigs in the early days of her career, Lady Gaga would call venues and pretend to be her own manager, believing that this would have more influence than calling as an artist. Today, her fame does the talking, and she was even named one of *Time* magazine's 100 most influential people in the world in 2010 and again in 2019.

In 2014, Lady Gaga went on a late-night talk show and invited the entire audience to a concert after the show. Which talk show was it?

———

a) *Late Show with David Letterman*

b) *Late Night with Jimmy Fallon*

c) *Jimmy Kimmel Live!*

You have to be unique, and different, and shine in your own way.

LADY GAGA

DID YOU KNOW...

Growing up, Lady Gaga's father owned a company that installed Wi-Fi systems in hotels, and her mother was a vice president at Verizon Communications. Driven by her creativity and love of performing, the singer forged her own path a world away from her parents' careers.

Lady Gaga was the headlining act during the Super Bowl halftime show in which year?

---

a) 2011

b) 2015

c) 2017

IF I COULD TELL THEM ANYTHING,

IT WOULD BE THAT THE WHOLE *YOU* MATTERS.

LADY GAGA

DID YOU KNOW...

In 2017, Lady Gaga became the first female brand ambassador for the luxury watch brand Tudor. Over the years, she has been involved in endorsing a number of other brands, including Tiffany & Co, Apple Music, Versace and Dom Pérignon.

At which former US president's sixty-fifth birthday celebration did Lady Gaga perform?

———

a) Bill Clinton
b) Barack Obama
c) George W. Bush

IGNORE ALL HATRED AND CRITICISM. LIVE FOR WHAT YOU CREATE, AND DIE PROTECTING IT.

LADY GAGA

DID YOU KNOW...

Lady Gaga's reason for performing regularly in her underwear is because her grandmother has very poor vision and can only make out lighter parts of her body, such as her skin and hair. She told Gaga, "I can see you, because you have no pants on."

In which MTV reality show did Lady Gaga briefly appear in 2008?

---

a) *Punk'd*
b) *The Hills*
c) *Jersey Shore*

I'm at a place in my life where I just want to feel like myself in clothes. Whatever that means.

LADY GAGA

DID YOU KNOW...

In 2011, Lady Gaga won an injunction at the High Court in London to stop the Moshi Monsters online game from releasing a single using an animated character called Lady Goo Goo which was inspired by the singer. The character already had a parody song called "Peppy-razzi" but the ruling banned the company from releasing any further music using Lady Gaga's likeness.

In which early 2000s teen drama series did Lady Gaga make a cameo appearance, in an episode called "The Last Days of Disco Stick"?

———

a) *Gossip Girl*

b) *One Tree Hill*

c) *The O.C.*

WHOEVER'S LISTENING: I LOVE YOU,

AND IF YOU'RE IN PAIN, I PROMISE YOU IT WILL GET BETTER.

LADY GAGA

DID YOU KNOW...

After breaking her hip, Lady Gaga was diagnosed with fibromyalgia, a disorder that causes chronic pain. She documented her struggles with the condition in her documentary film, *Gaga: Five Foot Two*. More recently, the singer said, "It's very under control. It took over my life for a long time, but I'm 95 per cent better."

How long does Lady Gaga say it took her to write "Born This Way"?

———

a) Ten minutes

b) One day

c) Ten days

IF I WORRIED ABOUT EVERYTHING THAT EVERYONE SAID, I WOULD NOT BE A GOOD ARTIST.

LADY GAGA

DID YOU KNOW...

For the 2012 Batman film, *The Dark Knight Rises*, Lady Gaga was briefly considered for the role of Selina Kyle, also known as Catwoman. Natalie Portman, Keira Knightley and Blake Lively were also considered. While Lady Gaga made the longlist, ultimately the role went to actress Anne Hathaway.

Growing up, Lady Gaga's younger sister, Natali, was nicknamed after an animal. Lady Gaga has this animal tattooed above her left elbow. What is it?

---

a) A bumblebee
b) A mouse
c) A cat

People will always talk, so let's give them something to talk about.

LADY GAGA

DID YOU KNOW...

While filming *House of Gucci*, Lady Gaga embraced method acting and lived as Patrizia Reggiani (ex-wife of fashion designer Maurizio Gucci) for around a year and a half. She spoke with an accent for nine months, even off camera. She said in an interview with *Vogue*, "I never broke. I stayed with her."

Actor Alexander Skarsgård appears as Lady Gaga's love interest in which music video?

---

a) "Paparazzi"

b) "Bad Romance"

c) "Poker Face"

YOU HAVE TO STOP CRYING,

AND YOU HAVE TO GO KICK SOME ASS.

LADY GAGA

DID YOU KNOW...

Both of the characters Lady Gaga plays in the *American Horror Story* anthology series are immortal beings. In the fifth season, *Hotel*, she played the vampire-esque role of Elizabeth Johnson, otherwise known as The Countess, who carries a blood virus. In the sixth season, *Roanoke*, she played an ancient witch named Scáthach.

Which TV character did Lady Gaga take along to the 2009 MTV Video Music Awards as her date?

———

a) Big Bird

b) Barney the dinosaur

c) Kermit the Frog

FAMILY – IT'S LIKE THE ROOTS OF THE TREE. THEY GROW LONG, AND SOMETIMES THEY'RE MANGLED, AND SOMETIMES THEY'RE FULL WITH WATER, AND SOMETIMES THEY'RE THIRSTY.

LADY GAGA

DID YOU KNOW...

Lady Gaga's 2016 album, *Joanne*, is named so after her aunt who passed away from lupus in 1974. Joanne is also one of Lady Gaga's middle names, given to her in honour of her late aunt. The lyrics of the song "Joanne" are about her aunt's death from the perspective of Lady Gaga's family.

In the video for the song "Judas", what notable religious figure did Lady Gaga play?

a) Mary Magdalene

b) Mother Teresa

c) Eve

If you don't have any shadows you're not in the light.

LADY GAGA

DID YOU KNOW...

At the time of Lady Gaga's Super Bowl halftime show in 2017, it was officially the third most-watched Super Bowl halftime show of all time. The performance earned her an Emmy nomination for Outstanding Special Class Program, and CBS Sports called her show the second-best Super Bowl halftime show in history.

At which 2010 award show did Lady Gaga wear the now iconic meat dress?

---

a) Golden Globes

b) Grammy Awards

c) MTV Video Music Awards

ART IS A LOT OF THINGS AND THAT'S PART OF THE JOY OF IT TO ME –

THAT IT COULD BE WHATEVER I WANT.

LADY GAGA

DID YOU KNOW...

One of Lady Gaga's early signature headpieces was a bow made out of hair, which was said to be inspired by the animated character Hello Kitty. It was first worn in the "Poker Face" video, but she was regularly seen with it many times after, such as the Nokia 5800 launch party in 2009. Bows also featured in a miniature version at the 2019 Met Gala, and in 2025 she paid homage to her iconic look with some leather bows for the release of her album *Mayhem*.

What was the name of Lady Gaga's male alter ego created during her 2010 "Born This Way" era?

———

a) Alejandro Paparazzi

b) Larry Gaga

c) Jo Calderone

SOMETIMES IN LIFE YOU DON'T ALWAYS FEEL LIKE A WINNER, BUT THAT DOESN'T MEAN YOU'RE NOT A WINNER.

LADY GAGA

DID YOU KNOW...

Lady Gaga has said in the past that she suffers from hair loss due to years of dyeing her hair platinum blonde. This might have been the catalyst for her 2025 hair transformation during her *Mayhem* album era, which involved her acquiring a blunt fringe and a more natural brunette shade.

On which album cover is Lady Gaga pictured fused with a motorcycle?

---

a) *Artpop*

b) *Born This Way*

c) *Mayhem*

Nobody can define you but you.

LADY GAGA

DID YOU KNOW...

When Lady Gaga was studying at New York University, someone created a Facebook group called "Stefani Germanotta, you will never be famous". She used this to fuel her passion and drive, saying: "This is why you can't give up when people doubt you or put you down – gotta keep going."

An original song written and performed by Lady Gaga, called "Hold My Hand", appears on the soundtrack for which 2022 Hollywood movie starring Tom Cruise?

———

a) *Mission: Impossible – Dead Reckoning Part One*

b) *Jurassic World: Dominion*

c) *Top Gun: Maverick*

I WANT PEOPLE TO WALK AROUND DELUSIONAL

ABOUT HOW GREAT THEY CAN BE.

LADY GAGA

DID YOU KNOW...

In 2011, Lady Gaga debuted a new look that appeared to be sharp, protruding bones from her cheeks, forehead and shoulders. Although she has never clarified whether or not the body modifications were really implanted under her skin, it is thought that they were simply temporary prosthetics. Regardless, they caused quite a stir!

In what year did Lady Gaga sing the US national anthem at the Super Bowl?

———

a) 2013

b) 2016

c) 2017

I USED TO ALWAYS BE LIKE, *BUT WHO'S GONNA HAVE MY BACK?!* AND NOW I'M LIKE, I'VE GOT MY BACK.

LADY GAGA

DID YOU KNOW...

Lady Gaga is famous enough to have had not one, not two, but 19 species of fern named after her! They include *G. germanotta*, which honours her last name, and *G. monstraparva*, which honours her fans – her Little Monsters. The recently discovered fern species also have a DNA sequence that spells out GAGA.

Lady Gaga's debut album was released by Interscope Records and KonLive Distribution in 2007. Which famous RnB singer owned KonLive Distribution?

---

a) Beyoncé

b) Usher

c) Akon

Don't ignore even the smallest glimmer of passion in your soul, run towards it with everything you have.

LADY GAGA

DID YOU KNOW...

Lady Gaga's fiancé Michael Polansky is said to have co-written seven songs on her 2025 album, *Mayhem*. She revealed that over 50 songs were written and recorded in total, which she narrowed down to just 14 for the standard edition of the album.

What was the name of Lady Gaga's Las Vegas concert residency at Park MGM's Dolby Live (formerly the MGM Park Theater)?

---

a) Lady Gaga Enigma + Ballads on Piano

b) Lady Gaga Monster + Jazz & Piano

c) Lady Gaga Enigma + Jazz & Piano

I DON'T WANT TO MAKE MONEY;

I WANT TO MAKE A DIFFERENCE.

LADY GAGA

DID YOU KNOW...

When she was 17, Lady Gaga used a fake ID to get her first tattoo, a treble clef on her lower back, much to the dismay of her family. Years later, while getting a tattoo of roses by renowned tattoo artist Kat Von D, she said: "When I got the first one they had a heart attack."

At which president's inauguration did Lady Gaga sing the US national anthem?

———

a) Donald Trump

b) Joe Biden

c) Barack Obama

WHEN I SAY TO YOU, THERE IS NOBODY LIKE ME, AND THERE NEVER WAS, THAT IS A STATEMENT I WANT EVERY WOMAN TO FEEL.

LADY GAGA

DID YOU KNOW...

In 2011, based on record sales and social media metrics, *Rolling Stone* named Lady Gaga the "Queen of Pop", and in 2012, she was ranked fourth on the VH1 list of Greatest Women in Music. She continues to make waves today, and as recently as 2025, was honoured with the Innovator Award at the iHeartRadio Music Awards for her role as a "modern day artist innovator".

For which movie performance did Lady Gaga win an Oscar, a Grammy, a BAFTA and a Golden Globe in a single year?

---

a) *House of Gucci*

b) *Joker: Folie à Deux*

c) *A Star Is Born*

Some people are just born stars — you either have it or you haven't, and I was definitely born one.

LADY GAGA

FINAL WORD

Abracadabra… now you're ready to embrace your inner warrior queen and become what you were born to be: Lady Gaga's biggest fan! Leave your friends speechless with your newfound knowledge of this legendary pop star and return to her inspiring quotes again and again to top up your confidence and self-love.

Any time you need a dose of Mother Monster to cure your disease, you'll find it waiting for you right here. Enjoy geeking out over Gaga, Little Monster!

ANSWERS

8. c	47. c
11. b	50. c
14. a	53. a
17. b	56. b
20. c	59. a
23. a	62. a
26. a	65. c
29. b	68. b
32. a	71. a
35. c	74. c
38. a	77. b
41. c	80. a
44. b	83. b

86. c	122. a
89. a	125. c
92. c	128. a
95. a	131. c
98. b	134. c
101. a	137. b
104. c	140. c
107. a	143. b
110. b	146. c
113. a	149. c
116. a	152. b
119. b	155. c

Have you enjoyed this book? If so, find us on Facebook at Summersdale Publishers, on Twitter/X at @Summersdale and on Instagram, TikTok and Bluesky at @summersdalebooks and get in touch. We'd love to hear from you!

www.summersdale.com

IMAGE CREDITS

Cross © 4LUCK/Shutterstock.com;
Glasses © top dog/Shutterstock.com;
Guitar © Vilmos Varga/Shutterstock.com;
Hand © Salome Bitsadze/Shutterstock.com;
Hat © Alpha Factory Std/Shutterstock.com;
Lightning © AAVAA/Shutterstock.com;
Stars © AspctStyle/Shutterstock.com